ARE YOU
WHO YOU
WANT 2 BE?

ARE YOU WHO YOU WANT 2 BE?

TRUST *your* INTUITION

SHAKEERA V. FORREST

authorHOUSE®

AuthorHouse™
1663 Liberty Drive
Bloomington, IN 47403
www.authorhouse.com
Phone: 1-800-839-8640

Published by AuthorHouse   01/28/2013

ISBN: 978-1-4772-8877-1 (sc)
ISBN: 978-1-4772-6726-4 (hc)
ISBN: 978-1-4772-8878-8 (e)

Library of Congress Control Number: 2012921605

In memory of **Vestine Paris Searles**. You left fingerprints of grace in my life. You shall not be forgotten.

Shakeera Forrest, at 30 years old is an accomplished mother, wife and entrepreneur in Atlanta, Georgia. Shakeera holds a Masters degree in Accounting and is currently pursuing her PHD in business with an emphasis in Marketing. Although she is passionate about many things her family and the legacy she leaves behind to her children are paramount in her life. She believes above all for all of us to make a positive change to ourselves, our country and our world thus leaving them better than we found them. Please feel free to join my discussion on Facebook (www.facebook.com/pages/Are-You-Who-You-Want-to-Be/407101279987) or follow Shakeera (@Everknowing1) on Twitter.

Grateful Appreciation Goes To:

My family—Rashaun Forrest, my husband, my best friend, my life coach. Thank you for always supporting me and not letting me deter away from my dreams. Love you forever! My children who I adore so much, Caleb Cardain, Kendall Summer, and Isis Milan who are one of the reasons why I am a strong woman today. Love you and always refer to this book if you ever need guidance. Be courageous and venture out into our world. Become the person, who you want to be! A generous appreciation goes to my siblings Torrey, Shatifa, Sabrina, Terence, and Denise who were a significant part of my growth during this time. Shatifa, you know exactly what to say to brighten my day. My uncles, aunts, nieces, nephews and cousins, I Love you all so much! Family is important!

My friends—Jessica Brown you were the first to believe in this vision! We have prayed countless times, and I am proud to say those things have come into fruition. Thanks! Alexander Hogan, Angela Elam, Brigitte Gunby, Charmaine Alexander, Denise Edwards, Krystal Jones, Michelle Guzman, Nichelle Wilson, my friend of 13 years Nika West, Starlat Ridgeway, and Yolanda Moore all gave me the courage needed to continue this journey. When I need to pick up the phone to cry, laugh or whatever I decide, you always listen. I love you all! Thanks for support, as I have finally finished!

My mentors—I would like to give a special thanks to New Life Christian Center in Augusta, GA! Pastor Bryan & Rhonda Matthews Rock!

"Your time is limited, so don't waste it living someone else's life. Do not be trapped by dogma—which is living with the results of other people's thinking. Do not let the noise of other's opinions drown out your own inner voice. And most important, have the courage to follow your heart and intuition. They somehow already know what you truly want to become. Everything else is secondary."

~ Steve Jobs

CONTENTS

As I held her hands, I said I love you. She squeezed my hand with all her might as a way to tell me the same. Those were my last words to my mother. After years of battling cancer, my mother passed away throughout the night. Shatifa, my sister, said she felt her spirit hovering over her body after she died. My world has never been the same since that dreadful day. I now reflect back upon the moments that were dear to my heart as a way to cope.

My mother didn't provide me with any large assets or wealth, but she did endow me with a courageous heart, knowledge of how to create positive social change, the ability to succeed despite challenging circumstances, willingness to strive for excellence, faith to believe that good things come to those that wait patiently, how to make ends meet when financial resources are sparse, and most importantly to treat others as I would like to be treated.

I was 12 years of age when my mother met her maker. I was two years old when my father departed his life. Currently, as a 30-year-old woman, I believe without any doubt that God filled the gaps when needed throughout my life. As a teenager, I knew if I wanted to conquer my dreams I would have to press in for things I wanted to come into fruition. I had to embrace and enjoy all the struggles I endured to make a better tomorrow. I matured earlier than most and lacked having a family to support me. In my younger days when I graduated high school, college, got married had a baby, etc very few family members attended. I say few because I come from a very large family and only around 10-15 people would show. Moreover, that is a generous number.

I moved from Lincolnton, GA to Augusta, GA, to Lexington, NC, back to Lincolnton, GA during grade school. I was in many different homes during this transition and realized then that every family has some sort of dysfunction. After graduating high school, I anticipated getting out the small town where I was raised the majority of my life with a population of 1,566. This diminutive town had only one traffic light, two gas stations, and one grocery store. I refused to go to a prom and joined few extracurricular activities to avoid being social.

During my senior year in high school I only applied to one college, Clark Atlanta University. I had made plans to attend and room with Nichelle Wilson, a good friend from grade school. Unfortunately, there was a waiting list for room and boarding which resulted in having to find shelter off campus. This was not an option for me, as I could not afford to make this conversion. Still not completely giving up, I went to a local college where I planned to complete my core courses until I was lifted off the waiting list. College life was not peaches and cream for me, especially with no income. There were times when I washed my own clothes out by hand and practically starved because of the lack of finances. Every weekend most students had resources to go home with family members or hang out within the city. Since I did not have this luxury, I would leave campus with my boyfriend. I eventually became pregnant at the age of 19. I contemplated if I needed to have this child at such an early age without the means of taking care of him financially. I am so happy I gave birth to an 8 lb 12 oz little boy named Caleb. He has been a guiding light on why I have spiritus (Latin for the breath of life). Before having my son, my life did not have substance. Later, I had another 8 lb child by the name of Kendall Summer. In addition, most recently, in 2012, I had a baby girl by the name of Isis Milan.

Throughout my life, I have dealt with many situations that seemed like would result in failure. However, with a strong mind, body, and soul I have pushed through more than imagined. In this book, I will give details of some circumstances that occurred that might help you get out of your funk and bring heaven to your doorstep. Embrace change and know that this precious time we have here on Earth is limited. Make the best decisions to have the best life imagined! If you have no family, friends, money, education, or whatever else you "think" you may need to succeed, this book will be an excellent read. **Enjoy!**

Chapter 1

You Are Essential

I struggled with knowing that my life had purpose. Often times I imagined walking in front of a tractor trailer to end it all. That negative mindset led me back at square one in life, which was nowhere. You have to grab hold of something or someone that has substance to focus on who you are and want to become. Over the years, I was blessed enough to have friends and meet strangers that spoke life over me to get me out of my rut. I also gained the strength to believe that I could fulfill my dreams if I applied myself and give everything my all. So today, there is no stopping what I can and will do! If I can think it, I can do it! I challenge you, as you read this book to have an open heart and optimistic mindset so you can reach inside, pull out your junk, display it, and deal with it! Everyone has demons in their life that they deal with. Just make sure you remember that trials and tribulations help shape who you are.

First, we are not perfect but we can strive to become better. Each day when you get out of your bed, think of a reason why you should smile. No day should be a bad day. We are all born with a divine purpose to fulfill. You have a significant position in heavenly places. Before we entered into our mother's womb, we were each made unique in so many ways. God has a special blueprint designed for every person that walks the face of this Earth. Trust in the position God gave you.

> *For he chose us in him before the creation*
> *of the world to be holy and blameless in his*
> *sight. In love, he predestined us to be*
> *adopted as his sons through Jesus Christ, in*
> *accordance with his pleasure and will to the*
> *praise of his glorious grace, which he has*
> *freely given us in the One he loves.*
>
> Ephesians 1:4-6 NIV

Let us get on one accord before we go any further. Please pray with me. "Father God who sits on the throne, I ask that you come into my heart and cleanse my mind, body and soul. I ask that you forgive me for my iniquities that I have committed, whether knowingly or unknowingly. Lord, I repent of all my sins because it is only I who sins against you. Wash me in the blood of the Lamb and bless me with wisdom and understanding so that I may become more like Jesus. Amen." If you prayed sincerely know, that God heard you and is more than ready to bless you with more than you can ever imagine.

God gave us free will to choose life over death. We are our own competition in this race here on Earth. Children grow up not knowing what they want to do with their lives because they are not positioned for their future. Do what is in your heart because that is where God implants our purpose before we are born. My ultimate goal for readers is to gain knowledge on how to find out what your life assignment is. Your calling here on Earth will determine how you will live your life. Instead of going down the road most pass through, go the way few travel.

> *Enter through the narrow gate. For wide*
> *is the gate and abroad is the road that*
> *leads to destruction, and many enter*
> *through it.*
>
> Matthew 7:13 NIV

You cannot solely decide who you are or who you want to be. Amazingly, God has already worked that out. Building a strong relationship with the Father ensures that you are a child of God that cannot be moved. We grow into our calling and I personally believe the reason we do not know it by instinct is that we would not know how to complete the assignment with our natural sense.

> *Therefore, I urge you brothers, in view of*
> *God's mercy, to offer your bodies as living*
> *sacrifices, holy and pleasing to God—this is*
> *a spiritual act of worship. Do not conform*
> *any longer to the pattern of this world, but be*
> *transformed by the renewing of your mind.*
> *Then you will be able to test and approve*
> *what God's will is—his good, pleasing and*
> *perfect will.*
>
> Romans 12:1-2 NIV

Every purpose contributes to the ultimate goal in our world. Every contribution that you make in your life has an impact on your local community, where good or bad. When missions are aborted, the purpose for our lives is as well. Stepping aside from religion, aren't you happier when you are carrying out your dreams? I am sure you feel essential when doing so.

There are several perspectives on the meaning of life that each one of us holds to be true. We cannot fault anyone for what individuals believe in. Whatever your spiritual and religious beliefs are, you still have a purpose in life. I researched and included some of the thoughts of others on the meaning of life that follows this section.

According to Seligman (2002) science may or may not be able to tell us what is of essential value in life (and various materialist philosophies such as dialectical materialism challenge the very idea of an absolute value or meaning of life), but some studies definitely bear on aspects of the question: researchers in positive psychology (and, earlier and less rigorously, in humanistic psychology) study factors that lead to life satisfaction, full engagement in activities, making a fuller contribution by utilizing one's personal strengths, and meaning based on investing in something larger than the self. (Seligman, 2002).

Baumeister and Vohs (2002) have synthesized four factors. When people are asked, the more they report each of these four factors being fulfilled, the more meaningful their lives feel:

1. **Purpose**—this could be living happily ever after, going to heaven or even (whisper it) found at work. Whatever it is, meaning in life comes from reaching goals and feeling

fulfilled. Even though fulfillment is hard to achieve because the state fades, people need purpose.

2. **Values**—people need a moral structure to work out what is right and what is wrong. There are plenty to choose from: some come from religion, others from philosophy and still others from your friends and family.

3. **Efficacy**—people want to make a difference and have some control over their environment. Without that, the meaning of life is reduced.

4. **Self-worth**—we all want to feel we're good and worthwhile people. We can do this individually or by hitching ourselves to a worthy cause. Either way we need to be able to view ourselves in a positive light (Baumeister & Vohs 2002).

There was a study conducted to investigate **purpose** in **life** in relation to psychological well-being, social relations, and physical and psychological symptoms among very old women (n = 120) and men (n = 69). Their **purpose** in **life** was evaluated using the **Purpose** in **Life** (PIL) scale. Women scored lower on this PIL scale than men (102 vs.108 p = .0.013). Regression analysis was used to estimate influencing factors on the PIL score. Determinants for **purpose** in **life** did not differ between the men and women, except for musculoskeletal symptoms. Attitude toward own aging had the strongest relation to PIL scores for both men and women; to have family to talk to was also important, as were musculoskeletal symptoms, for women. The study indicates that the very old people studied were feeling indecisive about their **purpose** in **life** and that feelings are linked with poorer psychological health. For this reason, the **purpose** in **life** must be discussed and taken into consideration in the care of the elderly (Hedberg, Gustafson, & Brulin 2010).

If you cannot recognize him and his works, then it makes you an easy target and allows distractions to enter into your lives. Once you realize that the devil has already been defeated then you will know that you can do whatever you set your mind to. Like Paul from the New Testament said, "Make sure you hit THE mark and not just A mark." Do not go through life just making decisions based off of your own desires. Notice it says all your ways acknowledge him, not just 90% needs to be considered.

> *Trust in the Lord with all your heart and lean*
> *not to your own understanding; in all ways*
> *acknowledge him, and he will make your*
> *paths straight.*
>
> Proverbs 3:5-6

When Jesus died on the cross for our sins and ascended into the Heavens with our Father, he left us with instruction of how to live a healthy life. His spirit tells us which way to go, what to say and convicts us when we are doing things that are out of line with God's word. Webster's dictionary states that God is the supreme or ultimate reality, the Being perfect in power, wisdom, and goodness who is worshipped as a creator and ruler of the universe. The enemy has already been defeated and we need to put all of our addictions, sicknesses, hatred, negative attitudes, and all other ugliest on the cross.

You have not chosen me, but I have
chosen you and appointed you to go and
bear fruit—fruit that will last. Then the
Father will give you whatever you ask
in my name.

John 15:16 NIV

Who you are in Christ determines your reasoning of existence. On your journey, know that you can be shipwrecked in the will of God. Sometimes we think when God allows us to go through difficulties we are outside of his perfect will. Just because we are in the perfect will of God, doesn't mean everything will be perfect. Also, remember we have free will. This is what deters many from becoming who they want to be. The choices you make dictate your future.

Be very careful, then, how you live—not
as unwise but as wise, making the most of
every opportunity, because the days are evil.
Therefore, do not be foolish, but understand what
the Lord's will is.

Ephesians 5:15-17

Are there times when you feel alone? We all have those moments but by faith, you will also know he is with you at all times. Sometimes when you pray and you still do not feel his presence then pray even harder. God is in us so how can he leave us.

> *Be strong and courageous. Do not be*
> *afraid or terrified because of them,*
> *for the Lord your God goes with you;*
> *he will never leave you nor forsake you.*
> Deut 31:6 NIV

If God is with us, whom should we fear? Build your relationship with God by reading scriptures, meditating in him, by sincere prayers, ministering to others out of love, obeying God moment by moment, trust God in every detail of your life, and allow the Holy Spirit to direct your steps. When you are rooted in Christ even strong winds cannot knock you down. By hearing God's word builds your faith and building your faith strengthens your relationship with God.

No one can fill those empty spaces in your life. If you are in a relationship and you still feel alone then you may need a stronger relationship with God. If no one can make you happy or make you feel loved then you need the joy of the Lord. You have to literally find the joy within yourself. Relationships complement each other but God completes you. So whenever you feel lonely in any relationship go to God and ask him to fill those unfilled spaces.

When you build a relationship with God you are able to talk to him wherever you go. The best quality is he listens to everything you have to say. You have to do more than just hope and try. You have to believe and then you will receive. When you are hungry for God's presence do not get discouraged if you feel empty. Friend, he is right there with you and has been before you were born. Stop hoping and start believing today! Once we start believing that he is right there with us then that is when he will pour his spirit across the barrenness of your soul. After you find out that, you are in him and him in you, you will realize that it doesn't get any closer than that.

Do not let someone else's relationship with God predict how yours should be. God speaks to us differently. When you are faced with this accusation, know that it comes from the adversary. Some people have been to heaven and even soared with Jesus but blessed are those who believe without seeing. Sometimes God will appear in visions or give signs and wonders so that people will believe in him. Furthermore, once you build a strong relationship with God you will be the person God uses to show people his power. Learn how to fight the enemy and keep your relationship with God strong and healthy. God is always with us but it is good to go to him in prayer and meditation. Having a set time with God each day to worship and love him makes you even sharper. Live in it day by day. It takes discipline to pray diligently. Since God forgave us for all our sins then we must forgive each other so our Father can hear our prayers. If you do not know how to pray, always start with the Lord's Prayer.

> *Our Father in Heaven, hallowed by*
> *your name, your kingdom come, your*
> *will be done on Earth as it is in heaven.*
> *Give us today our daily bread. Forgive*
> *us for our debt, as we also forgive our*
> *debtors. And lead us not into temptation,*
> *but deliver us from the evil one. Amen.*

Every prayer will be different because you will encounter different obstacles in your life. Sometimes you can rest in him and just meditate during prayer. There will be other times when all you can do is sob. The most important aspect of prayer is actually meaning what you say. God answers heartfelt prayers. Sometimes you will have intense prayers which require you to get a little "attitude" about yourself. We cannot command God to do anything for us in the spirit but we can ask for it in Jesus name. God wants us to be happy and live on this Earth as if it were Heaven. Wow, did you receive that! God wants us to have Heaven here on Earth. When you go through Jesus, you can have whatever your heart desires. God has made this promise to us.

> *And I will do whatever you ask in*
> *my name, so that the Son may bring*
> *glory to the Father. You may ask me*
> *for anything in my name, and I will do it.*
> John 14:13-14

Overcoming the struggle to pray only comes by forming a habit. Just saying you will start to pray will never be enough. Praying in the shower and in the car going to work is excellent if you have a busy life. I find myself using my hour commute to work to pray several times out of week. Diligence pays in the kingdom of God. After praying, remember some of the desires will not be obtained suddenly. Never give up if you cannot see your prayers come into existence. He hears everything we ask and acts accordingly to grant the petition. We must remember to be patient while he works in the kingdom. If you give a child candy before dinner more than likely the child will not eat as much. The same happens with us when we receive things in the wrong timing. In order for us to remain strong in spirit, we must pray and wait. There will be certain steps taken to acquire the things your heart desires. All of our prayers are yes and amen if we are committed to him. Sometimes when we pray action does not immediately follow the request. God sometimes have things in store for us that are better than our own expectations. We need to thank God in advance for the blessings to come. Always pray and never give up or give in. Let us not kill our angels!

> *Now to him who is able to do immeasurably*
> *than all we ask or imagine, according to his*
> *power that is at work within us, to him be*
> *glory in the church and in Christ Jesus*
> *throughout all generations, for ever and ever! Amen.*
> Eph 3:20 NIV

Selfish prayers are one of the most common mistakes we make. We get caught up in our situations and only edify ourselves. If we would just start lifting others up in prayer in tribulations our problems would turn around quicker. Pray for our nation, local communities, schools, other countries and churches. The hand of God moves when you start practicing this. Israel is still God's holy nation. He said those who prayed for Israel would be blessed. God is bigger than all your problems. Everyone is going through something; believe me! There are no wrong ways to pray when you are a child of God. Hypocrites however, want to be observed. There are some individuals that pray to be seen by others. The only reward for this type of prayer is that you are acknowledged for having the spirit of life.

But when you pray, go into your room, close the
door and pray to your Father, who is unseen. Then
your Father, who sees you what is done in secret,
will reward you.

Matt 6:6

You must believe that God exists before you pray. Like gravity, you cannot see it, but you know it exists. Try jumping off a 100-foot building. Believe and ask God to help you with all your unbelief. Be sincere with God and he will show you that he is real! After he reveals himself to you, you will know that it is he. There is no one perfect but God. Atheists have a crucial dilemma with prayer because they do not believe in him. Take up the challenge and see that God lives. From experience, I can say he is genuine. Without God, there is nothing I could put my faith in and nothing in my life was would have substance. Furthermore, I would believe that the world came into existence on its own and we just somehow evolved. We are too perfect to have just evolved. Our intelligence is not equivalent to any other animal. We were created for purpose by God and for God.

Without faith it is impossible to please God,
because anyone who comes to him, must
believe he exists.

Heb 11:6

Let God know when you need him to perform miracles. Ask him to intervene and move in such a mighty way that every evil force against you has to flee. Ask God to open doors that lead to your destiny and close doors that distract you away from them. Recognize whom you belong to and asking God for things will be easy. Get in his word to get his will!

～ **Moment of Truth** ～

I will not be able to sugar coat my life and say I had someone there for me along the way the entire time. Unfortunately, I did not have a mentor I could call in my times of need. God was there. Day in and day out, I could call on him. This book is spiritual because I believe in God and his works. Without him, I would be nothing. During my life, my siblings and I have been through some traumatizing events. In fact, some of them were life changing. We did not want people to feel sorry for us and treat us like charity cases but usually that is what people gravitated towards. It got to the point where we would not discuss our background or excuse ourselves from a conversation to avoid this. I went from living with my mom, to my uncle, to my aunt, to another aunt, to cousins, and back with another aunt. My sister, Shatifa Searles and I split from our brother, Torrey Searles at a very young age. I can now see this is because my mother knew she had become ill and would not be able to take care of us all. I moved around a lot and because of it, Sabrina Suber was added to the trio. For some reason, she could relate to some of our mishaps (although she had both parents) and was there for us and she still is. And boy, this is where the fun started. We had so much fun growing up together. We all grew up to be very successful without parents. My brother Torrey graduated from West Point Academy and now has a beautiful family. My sister, Shatifa graduated from University of North Carolina at Chapel Hill and is in law school. She also has a stunning family. We can now discuss our family history without becoming so depressed. Furthermore, we use our situation as a tool to help others.

Chapter 2

Love

*"Love is composed of a single soul inhabiting
two bodies" ~ Aristotle*

There is no way you could even tip toe into who you want to be without love. To walk in your fullest with God, you must abide in his love. Love appears in the Bible several times. This lets us know that the most important aspect of life is to love. God is love and love is God. His love endures forever. The greatest commandment is to love God with all your mind, body, and soul. The next one is to love each other like you.

Love is what happens when a mother kisses her child before bed. Love happens when two become one. When a baby is born love is born. Love is when you hold hands. Love is when you pray to God. Love is also when those prayers are answered. Everything in your life stems back to love. Without love, our world would be in a worse condition. We are to love our enemies for they know not what they do. God created everyone to be loved and to be lovable.

If, you find it complex to love others there may be a crisis that could be linked to your past life. Believing in the world alone can give you low self-esteem. Know that you are worthy and full of value to God. God needs you to do what you are called to. You are of great importance. God wants the love to flow out so your light will shine. Negative people are drawn to the light because they are in total darkness. So let your light flow out like a river so others can see it can be done.

Forgiving others instantly is an act of love. In order to genuinely love, you must forgive others from the heart. Forgiving a person in your mind will not set you free from this bondage. You must be full of compassion and have a heart like Jesus to forgive. It sounds difficult, but it is simple. Once your mind is renewed, your heart will be transformed. When you find yourself dealing with the same issues but with different people you need to review yourself.

Here, are a few tips that helped me get through those trying times taught by Ed Traut. The first step is to write it down then confess it and finally never talk about it again. Do not remember it. Do not maintain unforgiven thoughts in your mind. Emotional needs drive you towards the wrong purpose for your life. Emotional distress is a clear fruit of negativity. Someone may have tried to kill you, but you must forgive that person. What I am getting at is no matter what a person does to you, you must forgive.

We should show our love through actions. It is easy to tell someone you love them. Actually showing it is another hurdle that has to be taken with sacrifices made. Jesus gave the ultimate sacrifice by dying on the cross. The least we can do is love each other unconditionally. The greatest blessings come from loving each other.

Dear children, let us not love with
words or tongue but with actions
and in truth.

1 John 16:18

⌁ **Moment of Truth** ⌁

Too many times, we mistake lust for love. I am guilty of this. I was in an abusive relationship for years. This person was verbally and physically abusive to me. As I look back, I can clearly see now it was not my fault. The abuser will make you believe that you are the problem. It becomes hard to leave an abusive relationship because you become broken and feel trapped. It is also hard to reach out to friends and family because you feel they will judge you instead of helping. This particular person lied so many times and convinced me that I was not living a life that was pleasing to God. Sadly, he was a minister. I started losing faith in who I was and what I had believed all my life about God. I was not motivated to fulfill any dreams and could barely take care of myself at this point.

My self-esteem dropped well beneath the average homeless person. I did not have the craving to eat. I was told that these things happened to me because I was not good enough, smart enough, pretty enough and all the other hurtful things he could think of. His ambition was to hurt me so he could have complete control over me. After a couple of years past, I had become someone who I did not know. We would get into arguments that led him to lashing out on me. After he mentally, emotionally, and physically drained me, he would apologize and buy gifts. He knew exactly what to do to make the pain disappear temporarily. The cycle repeated itself and worsened over the years. My last encounter with him was when he put a gun to my head and said I had one minute to live and what were my last words. At this point, I screamed for help and of course, no one came to my rescue. I was terrified and had so many thoughts racing through my mind. I was so upset that I had not left before it had gotten to this point. I was so disappointed that I did not have the will power to stop the cycle.

After reaching out to friends and church members for prayer, I defeated this darkness in my life. I am not proud nor do I enjoy reflecting upon these circumstances. However, when no one has the audacity to stand up and speak up, we all become a part of the problem. If you are in an abusive relationship of any sort, please reach out for help. I never thought I would go through any type of abuse. It can happen to anyone. Love is not hurtful. Love is patient and kind. If someone loves you, they will not physically or verbally abuse you on any level.

"Love addiction," or excessive and suffering romantic attachment to a love object, has been described in literature for centuries and appears in many different cultures. However, it has never undergone systematic study, in part because there is no recognized definition or diagnostic criteria. As a consequence, very little is known about its epidemiology, psychiatric comorbidity, neurobiology, or treatment. Animal studies and limited human research suggest that the brain mechanisms mediating "love addiction" are similar to those involved with substance dependence. At the present time, the scientific evidence is insufficient to place "love addiction" in any official diagnostic nomenclature, or to firmly classify it as a behavioral addiction or disorder of impulse control destined to be used by a wide variety of professionals. There is a risk of misunderstanding and "overmedicalizing" persons with such disorders. However, neurobiological and clinical research on the subject has already brought much to both fields of research and will probably continue to do so (Reynaud, Karila., Blecha & Benyamina 2010).

Chapter 3

Pondering & Wondering

What the mind can conceive and believe, the mind
can achieve. ~ Napoleon Hill

It all begins in your mind. A single thought can lead to action. Actions can either lead to creating positive change or cause undesirable situations. No one is exempt from having thoughts. The key is being able to control our imagination so that it does not control us.

Baumeister (2012) defines self-control as what people use to restrain their desires and impulses. More precisely, it can be understood as the capacity to override one response (and substitute another). It is largely synonymous with 'self-regulation', a term preferred by many researchers because of its greater precision. To regulate is to change; namely, change in the direction of some standard, some idea about how something could or should be.

Self-regulation thus means changing responses based on some rule, value or ideal. Most self-regulation occurs in one of four spheres. People regulate *thought*, such as trying to concentrate or shut an annoying tune out of their minds. They regulate *emotion and mood*, such as when trying to feel better. They regulate *impulse*, such as when resisting temptation. Moreover, they regulate *performance*, such as by trading off speed and accuracy, or persevering despite a discouraging failure (Baumeister, 2012).

No matter who you are or what your status is, God's desire is for us to be obedient. Your life will affect other's futures. Disobedience can influence others just as well and will change their destiny.

> *For just as through the disobedience*
> *of the one man the many were made*
> *sinners, so also through the obedience*
> *of the one man the many will be made*
> *righteous.*
>
> Rom 5:19 NIV

You can cause a storm to arise on others around you because of your rebelliousness. Some generational curses go without notice because of this. Your disobedience hinders what your children will receive. Why not let your children benefit from you doing the right things. Choose life so that your children will not suffer from your mistakes. If you want to live a prosperous life, then focus on being true to yourself and others.

Self-control has been called the 'moral muscle' because it provides the power to do what is right. Not surprisingly, virtue deteriorates quickly under ego depletion. Experimental studies have shown that people become more willing to cheat and steal when depleted (Mead et al., 2009).

Negativity keeps you from recognizing the blessings that God has in store for you. It blinds your eyes from the light. A baby comes out of the womb by going towards the light. Obstructiveness keeps you in total darkness. The darkness gets heavier and eventually you can feel like you are wearing it. Do not put yourself into situations where transgression may evolve. If you are not strong enough to help others in difficult situations, stay out of the problem. Remember you do not have to be there to make a difference, a prayer can be said anywhere.

Do not blame others for cause of your wrong doings. Purify yourself by removing the darkness in your innermost being. With one mind, one goal and one voice nothing is impossible. When peccadillo enters your body, it distorts your mind. Your subconscious mind should not play a role when making a decision. People use self-control quite frequently.

A recent study (Hofmann et al., in press) had 200 people wear beepers for a week, and at random intervals they were asked to report on whether they felt any desire, and if so how strongly, whether they tried to resist it, and how successful that resistance was. Out of 10,000 responses, 7000 desires were reported. Efforts at self-control were common: people reported resisting two out of every five desires. Thus, much of the average day is spent trying to control one's wants and needs. What's more, this resistance was often successful. With no resistance, people enacted 70 per cent of their desires; with resistance, the rate dropped to only 17 per cent.

The popular image of self-control and willpower still conforms to traditional ideas of the person using inner strength to fend off strong temptations and cope with crises. Yet increasingly the evidence is suggesting that the most successful people, and indeed those with the best self-control, spend relatively less time than others struggling with temptations and crises. Yes, willpower can be used for such things—but it can also be used to set up one's life to run smoothly to avoid those demands and problems.

Trait self-control has been especially successful at predicting performance at school and work, which depends less on the single heroic feat of will than on having steady, reliable work habits. Put another way, some people use their willpower to study all night before the exam, but others use it more effectively by keeping up with their work so they do not have to stay up all night at the last minute. If anything, they make sure to get a good night's sleep so they are well rested for the exam. Willpower may have an unappealing, Victorian reputation. However, it is simply a matter of using one's physical and mental energy to reach one's goals and get the most out of life. It is one of the most important human traits and a key to long-term success in life (Baumeister, 2012).

≈ **Moment of Truth** ≈

I have worked since I was 14 years of age and I have always taken my career very seriously. I worked at a particular company in Augusta, Georgia for four years and became a valuable asset to the company. I was the Senior Accountant and the CFO and I had an awesome relationship. Until I became pregnant, my day-to-day routines had become a science. I was a dedicated employee, working after hours and on weekends if needed. I also grew with the company with all the challenges that arose. The strategies that the company had in place did not give them a competitive advantage. The key to providing excellent and uncompromising levels of service is to develop relationships with customers. At this company, many clients were complaining about the service they received.

After the first three months, I had a miscarriage, which led me to be out of the office for a couple of weeks. When I returned I got back in the swing of things immediately. My manger was concerned and asked if I needed more time. He stated that we could try to plan becoming pregnant again and wished me the best. A couple of months later I became pregnant again. When I told him the news, he was not chipper about it as it had been in the past. Instead of saying congratulations, he said well what are we gonna do? I was thinking to myself you cannot be serious. This same person recently wished me success on becoming pregnant. The environment changed after this conversation and it remained awkward each day. I started having complications during the first trimester and I took some time off to get some rest.

My manager became so irritated with me taking time off to go to doctors visits that he secretly hired someone to do my job.

He said his objectives were not to fire me. He also added that he intended to tell me about the new person when he had more time. Right! Someone who did not believe it was I, of course. I secretly conducted an investigation to gather more details about the new kid on the block. I went directly to the source and asked her some questions that pertained to work. At the time, I handled the payroll so was able to get all the particulars needed for my inquiry. We both had a Bachelors in Accounting degree and 10 years of experience in the appropriate fields. I held a Masters of Accounting degree and she had a Masters of Business Administration degree. Her salary would be 20K more per year. The only problem with the scenario was that they needed me to train her. Give me a break!

After my findings, I presented it to the owners of the company. I was not content and asked to be compensated the same earnings or I would not train her. They could not consider the assessment I made. They repeatedly stated how disappointed they were of me and how I should be thankful that I even had a job in the first place. They went on to say that, they only hired me because I was a single mom going to school at night. I literally had become a charity case within 20 minutes despite my hard work. Some of the comments were very displeasing and discriminatory. I was asked why I became pregnant since I already had two kids and how do I plan to take care of them. I did not bend because of their unpleasant remarks. The problem was still at hand, and the ball was in my corner and they were highly upset. After two hours of negotiating, they told me to go home until they reached a decision.

The next morning when I returned to work, there was a paper lying on my desk. They asked me to provide all the passwords that I used to store confidential information. I released this information without a problem. I knew what was happening but I was not about to let them scamper over me. I had four men standing in front of me with demeaning attitudes. I was commanded to train the new person and do not ask any more questions. He said, "just do it!" I politely said that I would not train the person unless I received the same pay. Long story short, they became livid and I was terminated. They also supposed that I would not be able to find another job.

Sometimes in life, you have to stand up for yourself. I needed a job; however, I was not about to be walked over. In addition, you should not either! With the recent slowing of the economy, jobs were not plentiful, and many displaced workers were returning to school to train for a new career. I decided I wanted to find another job. I interviewed with a recruiter in August and it seemed like it was taking forever to get a call back. Eventually, I received a call and was asked to interview with a company in Alpharetta, GA in two days. Of course, I love challenges and agreed to come. I got the job as an A/R Specialist and moved in with Nichelle Wilson until I found a home. I was pregnant and away from the family for an entire month. Since then, I have received a promotion as a Financial Analyst. More recently, I got a promotion as a Forecast Analyst, which pays much more than the woman I was supposed to train at my former job.

Again, never let anyone keep you from your blessings. Destiny has its way of paving the road for you. Make the best decisions for you and your family. Do not be afraid that you will not make it if you step out of the boat. When there is no risk, there is no reward.

Chapter 4

Stay Optimistic

Having positive relationships are healthy for you. Do not waste time trying to satisfy individuals who are negative. Being a people pleaser will not get you far in life. I have learned this the hard way. Some individuals will purposely try to steal your time by burdening you with their issues consistently. Having optimistic relationships helps you determine your strengths and weaknesses. You can loose your focus when you have people wearing you down. Sometimes you have to rid all the dead weight off you. Do not be blind to see your surroundings. Self-evaluations are helpful; however, your company also needs a check-up. Be careful in choosing your acquaintances. Trouble will always call you but do not put yourself in it. Sometimes it is hard to explain to others that your life has changed. Often, you will find the closest people to you will choose to go astray.

⤙ **Moment of Truth** ⤚

I once had a woman borrow $100 from me and promised to return it by a certain date. Leading up to date, she assured me that she would give the money back in a timely manner. Long story short, when the day arrived she could not be found. When I finally talked the person, there was an excuse after an excuse. She finally met me after several attempts at a restaurant and gave me 25% of what she owed while she and her husband ordered $200 worth of food. I dismissed myself from dinner to save myself from trouble. Weeks later, I received calls to explain why she had not paid all the money and to reiterate that she was upset that I did not stay for the entire dinner. Finally, she came over and brought food as a gift with the funds. I was wondering why the money was in a plastic bag. It should not have been a surprise that she paid for food with the money she owed. Being myself, I did not make an immense deal out of the situation; instead, after she left I never answered the phone again. Be aware of people that are users and only want benefits for themselves out the relationship. Every relationship is a give and take. Keeping positive relationships sets an example for others to follow. People who encourage you to seek God are those that are valuable in helping you fulfill your calling.

Make sure you receive this message correctly. This does not indicate by any means to ignore dishonest people, because God still loves them also. What this does mean is that you should be cautious what company you keep. Just be careful in the conversations that you engage in. Some discussions are worth not getting involved in. Our speech should be full of grace. You have the power to change the atmosphere around you.

Ministries are birthed out of relationships. Collaborating with others in the body of Christ brings your flame to higher altitude. Unity with others is good because light is shown on weaknesses that need correction. Two or more can put ten thousand to flight.

Letting unhealthy relationships go can be challenging until you control your mind to do what is right. Either partner, whether male or female, should not control the other person. Keeping positive relationships sets an example for others to follow. People who encourage you to seek God are those that are valuable in helping you fulfill your calling.

Make sure you receive this message correctly. This does not indicate by any means to ignore bad people, because God still loves them also. What this does mean is that you should be cautious what company you keep. Just be careful in the conversations that you engage in. Some discussions are worth not getting involved in. Our speech should be full of grace. You have the power to change the atmosphere around you.

Ministries are birthed out of relationships. Collaborating with others in the body of Christ brings your flame to higher altitude. Unity with others is good because light is shown on weaknesses that need correction. Two or more can put ten thousand to flight.

Letting unhealthy relationships go can be challenging until you control your mind to do what is right. Either partner, whether male or female, should not control the other person.

Humility

> *"If I must boast, I will boast of the things*
> *that show my weakness" ~ II Cor 11:30*

Some people mistake having a high self-esteem with arrogance. While praying, Muslims level themselves with the ground and acknowledge their lowliness before Allah. We should do away with selfishness and pride to humble ourselves. "Compassion is hard if you do not have humility," says psychologist Jordan LaBouff of University of Maine. Let us review some ways in which being humble are expressed.

Be Appreciative

Starting with your life, be thankful for all your family, friends, source of revenue, education, health, wealth, having a peace of mind, shelter, and anything else that is dear to your heart. Once we reflect, we should realize that it takes humility to be thankful for all achievements and sustain a healthy lifestyle. God created this world and we are only a small fragment of it. Just think about when you want a promotion or a new job and then you actually obtain it. There is a process of getting to where you are today. Sometimes we become bored and stagnant within our positions and seek growth. Reaching one's potential is awesome especially if you are appreciative of your status. In essence, you are in your predicament because you chose to be; whether you like it or not. "Therefore it says, God opposes the proud but gives grace to the humble." James 4:6

Listen to Others

This is a weakness that I had growing up and unfortunately, I had to learn to the hard way. If we could listen more than we speak, we would be moving more towards becoming humble. This will entail getting rid of that "I know everything" mindset. Listening allows you to learn new things about others that can be beneficial in your life. For example, there may have been a time, where you were in a group setting (especially college) and there was always that one person who thought he had every scenario figured out. I am also sure there were times when he/she was wrong and it was a huge letdown for them. It is acceptable to be an expert in your field and help others but we must also be able to listen to others as well.

Do Not Be Judgmental

"Better is a person of humble standing who nevertheless has a servant, than one who pretends to be somebody important yet has no food." Proverbs 12:9

Such a powerful scripture! We all have our work cut out for us with this section. We all want to feel important and show that we have accomplished success in our lives and sometimes frown upon those that do not. Who established these standards in our society have been in place for many years and reasons. After slavery, diminished, black folk were able to get jobs and a decent education. With this opportunity, they also could afford nicer amenities that were not available to them during slavery. Nowadays, some African—Americans still feel that it is a huge success to have the American Dream. Other races and cultures have different experiences that have a huge impact on the importance of their success as well. Everyone must be open-minded and realize that we come from different lifestyles which helps determine who we are.

33

Being judgmental shows that we do not respect the other person and is not receptive to their ideas. This simply translates into having a closed mind.

Acknowledge the Help of Others

Make an effort to acknowledge that you did not get to where you are alone. During your lifetime, there will be people to counsel, encourage, critique, and assist you while striving for distinction. Humble people do not take credit for all of their success and are very compassionate about sharing this fact.

"Give to everyone what you owe them.
If you owe taxes, pay taxes; if you revenue, then revenue; if respect,
then respect; if honor, then honor." Romans 13:7

All of these action steps will facilitate us all to become more humble in life. After writing this section, I have realized how important it is to have continuous growth in this area. The best act of humility is when Jesus washed his disciple's feet. A man so powerful and honorable made a remarkable decision to show his meekness. A study conducted by Jordan Paul LaBouff shows that humble persons are more helpful than less humble persons. Evidence from three studies proves this to be true. According to LaBoff, Rowatt, Johnson, Tsang, & Willerton (2012), the connections between humility and other prosocial qualities led us to develop a *humility—helpfulness hypothesis*. In three studies, humble persons were more helpful than less humble persons were.

In Study 1, participants ($n = 117$) completed self-report measures of humility, the Big Five, and helpfulness. In Study 2, participants ($n = 90$) completed an implicit measure of humility and were presented with an unexpected opportunity to help someone in need. In Study 3, participants ($n = 103$) completed self-report and implicit measures of humility and were presented a similar helping opportunity. Humility and helpfulness correlated positively when personality and impression management were controlled. Humble participants helped more than did less humble participants even when agreeableness and desirable responding were statistically controlled. Further, implicit humility uniquely predicted helping behavior in an altruistic motivation condition.

> *"Darkness cannot drive out darkness.*
> *Only light can do that."* Martin Luther King Jr.

Hard Decisions

Never let anyone decide what is best for you or your family. Your situation will be unique since everyone has his or her own personality. Getting positive advice from others is healthy; however, it does not mean you are responsible for transforming your mindset. There are some people that want you to react a certain way to benefit them. Do not waiver when others make the grass seem so much greener on the other side; instead, nourish your grass more. Be careful of those who always have the best way to do things in your life. Keep your personality intact so that you will remain distinctive. I have seen many people that have the same mindset because of adaption to the environment. There will be thousands of decisions you will be faced with during a lifetime. Sometimes the hardest decisions made bring the greatest return.

Divorce

Unfortunately, this topic hits home with me, as I have experienced this dreadful dilemma. Divorce is a painful experience that a person can undergo during a lifetime. Prior to the 1970s, divorce was not an option for couples in comparison to now where it has become the norm.

The United States has the highest divorce rate by far. Italy has the lowest percentage in this analysis. The last census was taken in 2008. The data was family-based rather than household based. The good news about divorce here in the USA it that it has declined since 1980. The percentages of divorces in 1980 were at a high of 7.9% that fell to a 5.2% in 2008. Per Bindley (2012), since 2008, more studies have been conducted to show that marriages have lasted longer in the 21st century than they in the 1990's.

According to Center for Disease Control (CDC), the National Center for Health Statistics within the USA, Nevada had the highest marriage and divorces rates from 1990-2002. Massachusetts, on the other hand, had the lowest divorce rates during this time. There are many different reports and websites that contain information; conversely, these seemed the most credible.

Year	Marriages	Population	Rate per 1,000 total population
2010	2,096,000	308,745,538	6.8
2009	2,080,000	306,771,529	6.8
2008	2,157,000	304,093,966	7.1

Year	Marriages	Population	Rate per 1,000 total population
2007	2,197,000	301,231,207	7.3
2006[1]	2,193,000	294,077,247	7.5
2005	2,249,000	295,516,599	7.6
2004	2,279,000	292,805,298	7.8
2003	2,245,000	290,107,933	7.7
2002	2,290,000	287,625,193	8.0
2001	2,326,000	284,968,955	8.2
2000	2,315,000	281,421,906	8.2

Year	Divorces & annulments	Population	Rate per 1,000 total population
2010[1]	872,000	244,122,529	3.6
2009[1]	840,000	242,610,561	3.5
2008[1]	844,000	240,545,163	3.5
2007[1]	856,000	238,352,850	3.6
2006[1]	872,000	236,094,277	3.7
2005[1]	847,000	233,495,163	3.6
2004[2]	879,000	236,402,656	3.7
2003[3]	927,000	243,902,090	3.8
2002[4]	955,000	243,108,303	3.9
2001[5]	940,000	236,416,762	4.0
2000[5]	944,000	233,550,143	4.0

[1] Excludes data for California, Georgia, Hawaii, Indiana, Louisiana, and Minnesota.

[2] Excludes data for California, Georgia, Hawaii, Indiana, and Louisiana.

[3] Excludes data for California, Hawaii, Indiana, and Oklahoma.

[4] Excludes data for California, Indiana, and Oklahoma.

[5] Excludes data for California, Indiana, Louisiana, and Oklahoma.

Note: Rates for 2001-2009 have been revised and are based on intercensal population estimates from the 2000 and 2010 censuses. Populations for 2010 rates are based on the 2010 census.

Source: CDC/NCHS National Vital Statistics System.

Regardless, divorce stinks! Divorce should not be a win-win situation. When children are involved, it often makes the situation worse. Many individuals become unhappy in marriage and fault their mate. In reality, the person is unsatisfied with self and continues to be this way after the marriage is dissolved. I recommend seeking Godly advice before the final say so is made. Remember, it never hurts to do a self-evaluation. Now, the results may be a bit painful to see that you actually need work but it is rewarding.

From an emotional and psychological perspective, children need to have both parents in home. This may not be biological parents; nonetheless, it helps cultivate and teach them how to love and receive love. By both parents displaying a positive role, children can easily gravitate towards being more loving in relationships. Parents should be a role model for their children, as they will become the next generation.

"The way we talk to our children becomes their inner voice."
Peggy O'Mara

At one point in my life, it was very difficult to come to grips that I could not handle the circumstances as much as I thought I could. Some parents are focused on the physical well-being of the child and forget how important their psychological state is. Single parents become heavily involved with making sure food is on the table; shelter overhead, clothes on back that they do not have time for themselves. The health of a child's mind is highly imperative. I learned from experience when it comes to single parenting. This was a giant hurdle in my life that took determination to jump. By no means am I saying single parents cannot raise a child alone; rather, it is more beneficial for the child emotionally and psychologically to have both parents. The best way to find this out is by communicating with your child. Whether divorce was a factor in having a child or not, at the end of the day, it is harder to manage alone. Not many people want to face this or express this to others, but it is true.

Regardless of how a marriage ends, it always takes two people to agree to become married and one person to seek divorce. Just like politics and religion, this touchy subject causes a great deal of controversy. There are many aspects in regards to divorce that can handicap a family. A marriage can start in church but note it must go through the court system to end. As my mom would say, "things are so much harder to get out of than getting into." I encourage all readers to do your due diligence and educate yourself more on this topic if you are enduring this struggle.

Every divorce will have a unique situation I am sure. No one should throw stones at the two because of their decision. If that were the case, I would be dead already. Instead, learn from your mistakes and make things healthier.

Personally, I believe divorce rates are falling because people are choosing co habilitation. To me, this tells the child that commitment is not necessary in order to have a successful relationship. Kids are the product of their parents or whoever is responsible for their well-being. Regardless, children tend to do what their parents show. We do have some generation changes such as me that seek to find happiness in a more positive way.

Divorce has a negative ripple effect on more aspects of life than we probably notice. Each family has a detrimental effect on society. Some examples of the effects on divorced families are health and behavior problems, financial troubles, teen pregnancy, child abuse, new family members (stepparents, stepbrothers and sisters), crime, drug abuse, and higher dropout rates.

Going forward, let us make a collective effort to help save marriages and understand the true meaning before getting into a relationship that you will regret later.

Do not fight your battles from a human standpoint. Stop fighting against people because they are not the problem. There is a spiritual realm where demons and demonic powers exist. God and his angels protect you from these principalities. Let God fight all of your battles. Your tongue is like a double-edged sword.

Once you start receiving blessings and victory overcomes your life, watch out for the haters. Sometimes the people closest to you to will try to bring you down. Keep your eye on positive aspects of life. Use the best weapon that God gave us, the Holy Bible. For those that do not believe in the Bible, think of it this way. Most of the Bible contains positive passages. Try it!

You know no one ever wakes up with a Godly mind and intend to hurt you. Recognize that it comes from the enemy. People are continuously being used as bait to be a distraction in your life. Darkness comes and tries to steal your heart and fill it with unconstructiveness. With God in control, we will not receive more than we can bear. His yoke is easy and his burdens are light.

Put away perversity from your mouth;
keep corrupt talk far from your lips.

Let your eyes look straight ahead,
fix your gaze directly before you.
Make level paths for your feet and take
only ways that are firm. Do not swerve
to the right or left; keep your feet from evil.

Pro 4:24-27

Staying focused helps, you recognize the enemy. Do not let your conversations become distractions. Some people often love to strike an ungodly discussion with you to engage in polluted noise. Find peace in all your conversations so they will be meaningful. According to Webster's dictionary, a gossiper is a person who habitually reveals personal or sensational facts about others. Whether it is a rumor or a fact, no one should speak of another's situation without his or her presence. If you struggle with gossiping, one way is to fast from communication with others. Not saying you should go around and pronounce you are not talking to your friends but instead spend more time to yourself. Sometimes situations do not always need your opinion to be controlled. Avoid getting into meaningless conversations.

Chapter 5

Pick It Up Again

While traveling back home from Atlanta, Georgia God showed me an illustration of life. The weather was the worse it had been in years. It was snowing with a temperature around 33 degrees. While singing the gospels I noticed my oil light appear but I just kept going because I had already gotten an oil change recently. Suddenly my car started shaking and I tried slowing down but that did not work. Not knowing what to do, I pulled over almost causing accidents because of the blurred vision. I went to the nearest gas station in sight and looked under the hood. Everything looked okay so I checked the oil to find out that it was completely empty. It was freezing cold and the latch to hold the hood up was broken. I held up a 30 lb hood and poured oil into the car at the same time. After 20 minutes of torture, I returned on the journey. I was so excited because I thought the car only needed oil. I turned my music back up and praised God. Only getting five miles away, my car began to shake again. I thought I did not give the oil enough time to dispense throughout the car. I stopped at another gas station, turned off the car, and waited for another 20 minutes. I prayed that God would continue to give me traveling mercies and started back on the trip. The car went for approximately 15 miles this time before it started shaking. This being the third time, I already knew all I had to do was sit patiently for about 20 minutes. I figured if I kept stopping and going, I would eventually get home without calling a tow truck. By this time I had not seen the oil light appear so I knew that had caused the disaster. This came very repetitive the fourth time and I had to do something for the safety of other travelers and myself. After stopping again, I checked the transmission fluid to find that it was low as well. I added more oil and waited another 20 minutes before driving. As I got onto the highway, my car started to shake again. I knew that if I kept stopping it would take a day to get home. I did not want to drive at night in the snow. I just turned my hazard lights on and out of nowhere a pick-up truck pulling logs appeared and I followed it. He was going about 55 mph. I could maintain that speed and the people behind me would see the big truck before coming up too close. The car still was shaking but I just turned up the radio and sung praises to God. Sometimes it would be smooth sailing and other times it felt like I was on a vibrating roller coaster ride.

The moral of the story is that whatever the circumstances are in your life you have to keep picking it up when you fall. No matter how many times you fail, trust in God and he will get you to your destination safely. He will send people that you can follow to help you get to your destiny. Jesus spoke in parables and I went through that so he could show me that he still does. If I had gave up and called a tow truck, I would have wasted a lot of money and time. God will supernaturally cut corners for you to avoid disasters. During trials, you need to be patient and understand why God allowed you to be faced with that dilemma. Everything has purpose in the kingdom of God. The through trials and tribulations you go through mold you into who you are called to be. Without problems, you cannot grow to the potential that you were created for.

Do not think for once that you are living an indecent life if you are having trials and tribulations. Everyone has a devil in their lives that they deal with. No is perfect. Be sure to put a smile on your face even when the times get tough. Enjoy the struggle. Not everyone should know when you are going through. Jesus was persecuted on a daily basis. In addition, while doing so, remember that those who endure hardship will reap a harvest.

Friends, it's time to realize that we can never give up or give in to the things we want out of life. No matter what others say about you, continue your race. The harder it gets, the closer you are into becoming complete. We all grow each day and you are gradually becoming a stronger person. Confess your sins and pick it up again. Do not allow anyone to hold you down with condemnation.

Know the difference between condemnation and conviction. The Holy Spirit convicts while the enemy condemns. Sometimes it is hard to get back up again if you cannot tell the difference. The enemy condemns you which leads to depression and that is the key to destruction. The Holy Spirit convicts you only so you can better yourself and not hold you back. If you stay distracted, you will never get back up. The reason people stay depressed and idle for so long is that they are brainwashed into believing they cannot do anything to change their situation. This causes a major delay until you can get back on your feet. Which one are you? Do not let anything or anybody hold you back from what is in store for you.

When the pressure is on you, that is when you need to trust only in God. When you are tired of crying and you are still going through, keep pressing in. For he shall come to your cry and take you through the storm. Just hold on to his unfailing love. He will never let you down! Never give up, that is the plan the enemy has for you. Praise your way through the situations you are entangled in. Remember that God will help you pick it up again if you attempt to help yourself. Believe that you have power in yourself to pick it up again. Just as you have the power to walk you, also have the power to move mountains. God has a way of returning your attention back to him if you get off track. He will steer you in the way you must go. Being obedient is an automatic ticket to eternity.

Serve our God with all that you have and never give up. We do not know how long we will spend our lives here so that is enough to praise! Just believe him in your heart and you will come to know him even more than you already do. Your life is a divine setup, just knowing that is enough to make you change your way of living. Just never let go of what you believe. Keep it in your heart and in due time you will reap a harvest. The spirit of God is powerful! Rise within us Holy Spirit, so we can soar like eagles! Show your glory!

Sometimes in order to pick it up again you have to change your position. This may be physically relocating or a mindset change. Let the Holy Spirit lead you. Do not turn to friends for the direction God wants you to go. When you are going to another level, many will not understand. Only you will know the next step because it is already ordered. To get your breakthrough you must trust God with all your might that he knows what is best for you. It may hurt to change positions; however, you will receive everything you need and more to get your breakthrough! Just like a woman in labor, pain gives birth to life. It is easy to sit and look around at the world's living standards. Do not adapt to this universe but instead look beyond what this world offers and you will see eternal life ahead. You will receive the crown of righteousness from our Heavenly Father if you look beyond what the natural senses can display.

Of course, life gets hard sometimes but hang in there. Pick it up again and get on the path of righteousness. Do not be surprised if God himself push you where you need be. You will find yourself thinking, God why is this happening to me? You can be in his perfect will and long for more understanding of the situation, you are in. It is always so clear later to see the reasoning of circumstances. Maturing in Christ is not easy. We will be persecuted until the day we leave this Earth. The harder you press in, the harder the enemy will attack you. If you have on the full armor of God, he cannot have your mind, soul, or body. Stay in tune with the Holy Spirit to stay in his covenant.

Jesus was discriminated against all the way to the cross. He had nails punctured into his hands and we complain about the trials we face. He knew what was going to happen to him and he still did not resist. Therefore, with that said, just stand your ground and know that you are supposed to face problems. Do not try to run away from dilemmas because they will meet you wherever you go. Jump each hurdle, pass your test, swim through the valley, and when you get up again run even harder! Go beyond your expectations you have set for yourself.

We are God's precious gems and he does not want anyone to be left behind. Keep pressing in and your faith will take you to your next level. Press in like the woman with the issue of blood. She had so much faith that when she touched Jesus' garment she was instantly healed. She pressed through the crowd and was determined to receive her healing. We have to keep pushing through the pack as well to receive our blessings. God grants our petitions but we must put forth an effort to obtain them. You can't just sit around and expect Heaven to fall down on your lap without dedication.

Once you have picked it up again, keep the momentum. If you want to receive your miracle in a moment, just believe you will receive. Everything you want is ready to be given to you. God is waiting for us to believe. He wants us to understand the power that we have within ourselves. When this is revealed, the Heavens will shower you.

Do not turn around after you have made it this far. If you look back over your life, you will observe all the times you thought you were in danger and you were saved. All the times when no one else was there to be a shoulder to cry on, God was there. I am confident that there numerous times in your life where God showed up and showed out for you. Yes, we all have dull times in our lives, stuck in the desert. Did he bring the Isralites out of Egypt? Well, he can do the same for you and me. He is the same God now. Moses had to leave his wife and children to fulfill his purpose.

> *Consider it pure joy, my brothers, whenever*
> *you face trials of many kinds, because you*
> *know that the testing of your faith develops*
> *perseverance. Perseverance must finish its*
> *work so that you may be mature and complete,*
> *not lacking anything.*
>
> James 1:2-4 NIV

Pick it up and move forward. You must go through the storms for a new season.

If you dwell on the past, you will be caught back in it. Believe me I know this to be true. Declare that it is a new day everyday and watch your situation turn around. God loves you too much to leave you hanging. He is waiting for you to pick it up again to give him something to work with. He cannot do new a thing in you if you are still doing old things. Bring light into the world. Rise up and live so our Father in heaven can be glorified. He needs us to be the light of this world.

> *Forget the former things; do*
> *not dwell on the past.*
> *See, I am doing a new thing!*
> Isaiah 43:18

In addition, whatever you think you can do, you can. Take all the ideas in your mind and bring them into reality. He has someone in place already to help you along the way because he has implanted the ideas inside you. After reading this book, I want you to understand that you hold the answers in your heart. Trust yourself!

~~ **Moment of Truth** ~~

My husband and I became pregnant early 2011, and we were ecstatic. Although this pregnancy was unplanned, we were still anticipating the arrival of an angel from above. As you know, the first trimester is the hardest part of pregnancy (in my opinion) to manage. I had almost made it through the first trimester before I started experiencing complications. I went from having slight pains to spotting within a matter of weeks. I went to the doctor regularly, and everything was fine with the baby and I. Internally, I knew something was not quite right. I continued my daily regimens thinking it was a part of the first trimester. After a flight back from Dallas Texas, I knew something was off. I was busier than usual. We had just moved into our new home, and I was working on my doctoral studies. In fact, I did have several tasks to fulfill at this time in my life. After frequent complaints, my husband said to make an appointment with the gynecologist. He reassured me that everything was well and that it is a part of pregnancy.

Since I had two kids at the time, I had the experience to know something was wrong. I finally made it to the doctor, and he told me not to worry. He also added that the symptoms I was experiencing were normal. I left the doctor's appointment confused and happy. Yes, I know very mixed emotions. Refraining from any strenuous activities helped me overcome fears of a miscarriage. The spotting gradually became worse and led me back to the physician's office. At this point, I was certain something was erroneous, and I went back to seek answers for my condition from my doctor. Again, I was told to relax and rest since the baby was fine. However, at this appointment there was not a heartbeat. I had enough strength to trust the doctor's input and left away thinking I was being a bit hard on myself. We went home and celebrated our pregnancy once more until the next morning.

My life changed when I stepped out of my bed. I dreadful cramps in my lower back and was still spotting. That sick feeling that comes along with the first trimester vanished over night. I looked at myself in the mirror and sobbed for quite some time. I knew the baby was no longer alive. I cried before I knew! I asked my husband to take me to the doctor immediately. After calling the doctor's office, I became angry. They denied seeing me. I had so many feelings that overcame my body. I demanded to see the doctor. If I could not see him, I would go to the hospital.

After practically yelling at the nurses, I received a scheduled time. My husband still had faith that everything was satisfactory. I had never been so nervous in my lifetime. I was asked to change into the ultrasound attire, and as I lie on the table, all I could think of was that my baby might be dead. When the nurse came in and performed the ultrasound, I was shaking. The story unfolded by the look in her eyes. She rushed out the office to grab the doctor to confirm her findings. Most doctors are dumb to the fact that women experience great difficulty with pregnancy, but on this day I felt he truly cared. His words were, "Unfortunately, Mrs. Forrest, you have experienced a spontaneous abortion." I had no tears because I had cried before I knew. He sent me home to have a natural miscarriage. This turned into a disaster.

After a week, I decided to unwind and have some "me time". I had no idea having a natural miscarriage would lead me to an overnight stay in the hospital. I went from having heavy cramps to contractions to being in labor with the natural miscarriage. I almost bled to death and went to the hospital to receive a blood transfusion that I refused. I was in persistent pain for 12 hours without pain medication. I was in labor, and my body was not ejecting all of the remnants within the body. With help from an emergency physician, it was over finally. Physically, I had gone through the pain and came into realization that my body did what it needed to do to rid itself of all abnormalities. Emotionally, I felt as if my womanhood was robbed. I could not understand why my life had so many vicissitudes.

Time heals wounds! I felt 60% better within a few weeks with the help of my husband. Without him, this would have been very hard to overcome. I had come to grips with the fact that trials and tribulations can occur at any given time. We were trying to become pregnant, and two months later, we did. I had a healthy baby girl by the name of Isis Milan. Sometimes in life, we go through state of affairs that we do not understand but grow from. This was a hard time in my life, but I reached inside and pulled out magnitudes of strength to overcome this battle. Although I still have a scar from this, I can say God knows what is best for me. Pick it up again, keep running, pass the baton, and smile while doing so.

> *Blessed is the man who perseveres under trial,*
> *because when he has stood the test, he will*
> *receive the crown of life that God has promised*
> *to those who love him.*
>
> James 1:12 NIV

Chapter 6

Somewhere Over the Rainbow

*The city does not need the sun or
the moon to shine on it, for the
glory of God gives it light, and the
Lamb are its lamp. The nations will
walk by its light, and the kings of the
Earth will bring splendor into it. On
no day will its gates ever be shut, for
there will be no night there.*

Rev 21:23-25 NIV

Each day we have a chance to produce good fruit. When you breathe your last breath, you should be confident that your spirit would remain in God. Paradise is the full reward of a submissive life to God. Heaven is a place where you will never utter a complaint again. Jesus sits on the throne, and we will forever praise and worship him singing, "holy holy God Almighty, who was and is to come." You do not want to miss the honor of worshipping God. Entering into heaven is only the start of your afterlife. This is where you will live for infinity. Our fleshly minds cannot even comprehend the fullest of eternity. Eternity needs to be set in your heart so you will forever remember there is purpose for your being.

> *They will be his people, and God himself*
> *will be with them and be their God. He will*
> *wipe every tear from their eyes. There will*
> *be no more death or mourning or crying or*
> *pain, for the order of things has passed away.*
> Rev 21:3-4 NIV

This chapter should be what drives you to fulfill your calling. Knowing that one day we have to meet our maker is breathtaking. I do not know about you, but I want to hear job well done my friend. One day we all have to take account for our actions here on Earth. You never know when the end of the world is coming for you. Family and friends have left this world to be with the Creator. I believe we will be with them again.

Before your body goes into the grave be secure that God is your savior. Nobody will know when their last breath will be, and that is why we must stay on guard. Let us see each other on higher grounds. Therefore, we may not know when the world ends but your life can come crashing down at any time.

The book of Revelation was made known to John by an angel sent from God. God sent it to show all his servants what would soon take place. Much is revealed, and little is understood in the last chapter of the Bible. God does not want us to be afraid of dying because he holds the keys to death. Something that is for sure is that our bodies will die and return to dust while your spirit lives on.

We all have different opinions on where the spirit goes after death. Some believe we join Jesus, family members, and friends and live everlasting according to how we spend our lives here on Earth. Others believe that our spirit or energy within our body roams throughout the Earth and joins other spirits.

Take your mind away from the problems of the world. Meditate; visit a beach lake, etc. If you are lucky enough go to a Caribbean island. Do what it takes to get to a comfortable place so all that you have to do is breathe. Reflect on what you are doing and who you have become. Are you fulfilling all your aspirations? While you are in your quiet place, exhale, and think about the paradise you will enter after this life. If you mix the two, you will come up with a theory and purpose for your life. This technique requires some deep soul searching and to be brutally honest with self. It only involves you since this is your life. Be on track to becoming a better you. You will be so happy you did and others on the other side of the rainbow will too!

Somewhere Over the Rainbow

Somewhere over the rainbow you can see unlimited skies, if you follow it long enough it is said, you will find a pot of gold at the end of the run. I followed the rainbow in hopes to find such Luck. Spring buds in hope with every Sunrise…I am awakened in hopes of a brand new day and with every exhaling moment the winds whisper your name. Enthralled by constant feeling I look up to the one above, in prayer I kneel as I ask for this bud of hope and love. Spring buds in hope I am told, for with every spring everything new grows. I am truly looking forward to what this spring of life holds…

Enthralled by constant feeling I see myself smiling and laughing as I did once before. Why is this giddy smile plastered on my face for? A voice whispers to my ear and says "Be happy and do not try and comprehend why? Be happy…Let Go and let GOD" Somewhere over the rainbow dew drops dry and troubles disappear in the wake of an eye.

Spring buds in hope with every water that flows, birds that sing, of this wonderful day in Hope. The wind is blowing through my hair; the view peaceful and calm even with the water flowing from my eyes. So, I wipe the tears with my palm; a beautiful sight. It's an enchanted moment the Sun-shinning bright, birds singing in the distance, beavers strolling across the lake they come up and crawl under the fence.

The bright reflection from the sun sits across the lake, the rays burning warmly on my face. I look up to sky above, I see the rainbow and I know. I need to close my eyes and just let go. A gentle whisper of the wind brushes my face like a gentle kiss. Thinking of the past… No one can understand what I have been through in my life. I am enthralled by constant feeling to stay alive, to breath; the air just to survive. The world's harsh stare mean nothing to me now…What's in the past with secrets hidden and shadow casts. "I must Let Go and now Let GOD"

A Rendition to my dear dear friend of everlasting Life and Hope.

By Michelle Guzman

There are so many different perspectives on what actually happens after out body dies. Here are some experts from scientists and researchers about life after death. I think it is quite interesting to see what other individuals believe on this controversial topic.

The question of whether there is any life after death represents one of the most important philosophical topics. The dying process and the subjective experience of dying is a question of which very little is currently known. During the last decades, several clinical cases have been reported where patients described profound subjective experiences when near-**death**, a phenomenon called "near-**death** experience" (NDE). Recurring features in the accounts involving bright lights and tunnels have sometimes been interpreted as evidence of a new **life after death** (Agrillo, 2011).

In 1975, Raymond Moody published a book where the experiences of more than 100 people who had been close to death have been reported (Moody, 1975). Recurring features in their accounts included seeing a tunnel, a bright light, deceased relatives, a mystical being, entering a new domain, reaching a point of no return, a review of their lives as well as "out-of-body experiences" in which people described a feeling of separation from their bodies and the capacity to watch themselves from a point above (Agrillo, 2011).

Greyson and Bush (1996) classified several reports of unpleasant NDEs into three main categories: 1) the most common type includes similar features to the pleasurable type (i.e., out-of-body experience, movement through a tunnel or a light), but then people experience the features as frightening, probably due to feeling out of control of what was happening; 2) the second type included an acute awareness of nonexistence or being completely alone in an absolutely empty space; 3) the last type is less common and includes hellish imagery such as an ugly or foreboding landscape, demonic beings, annoying noises, and frightening animals.

Personally, I believe there is more to life somewhere over the rainbow. With our universe as bravura as it is, there is no way there is not more to see. Our world is splendid, wonderful, full of exciting lands to explore, and we enjoy it with those close to us. Moreover, to think it only gets better after we leave our physical bodies gives me the motivation to live a healthy life in all ways.

Whatever religions you believe in, at the end of the day we all are human and are all destined to be great. Religion has separated and controlled our behaviors for many years. The question is not whose religion is correct but who are we and what impact do we have on others? Are we living a pleasing life and what legacy are we leaving to the next generation?

What lies beyond what our human eye can see remains a mystery. We all have our perspective on death and the process thereafter. Who is right? No one can shed light on this, except God. We have to have faith that there is more to come outside of our lifetime.

We are just getting the technology to explore space, beneath our massive oceans, deserts, and rainforests. Imagine the things that have not been discovered in our lifetime. Generations from now, I believe, there will be complimentary trips to outer space. We only have a snippet of things to come after our lives are over here. Enjoy what you have here and celebrate when others pass on as they are entering into a paradise that rewards a worthy life! Fix your eyes on possessions that hold substance. Besides God, our imagination is the closest attribute that we have that provides us with vivid pictures of things to come.

So yes, I trust that somewhere over the rainbow lie no more trouble, heartaches, depression, worrisome hearts, poverty, starvation, and all other negativity that has held individuals back from becoming who they want to be. When I leave this world, I want to be remembered as the person who affected the lives of others' in a positive way. My parents may have died when I was young and I did have kids at an early age but I can look back and see that God showed up and showed out in my life. Nothing fell down in my lap since I have worked hard for everything I have. Many nights I have stayed up doing homework, ironing clothes, reading, writing, cleaning, and crying but it all pays off in the end. Making a difference starts with self. No one can get help if you need it most. Stay strong and focus on what you want to leave behind after your race. What is most important to you? What is your passion? You decide.

Trust in your gut and grab hold of what life actually means. Live your life as a representation of peace. Remain calm during the storms because the sun will shine on you again. Become the person who you want to be and do not let circumstances or others dictate what your passion is. So now, I will ask you, Are You Who You Want to Be?

Keera's Motivational Tips for Success:

1. **Write it Down:** To capture a vivid picture of things you want in life, you should keep a journal. Write down short and long-term goals, and refer back to this regularly to stay on track.

2. **Picture Your Future:** What do you see? Have you moved? Got a new job? Lost weight? Have you started your dream business?

3. **Visualize Your Past:** We should not reminiscence on the past frequently but it is okay to reflect upon how far you have come. What are you doing differently? Have you improved in your weak areas? This will assist you in staying on track for success.

4. **Go Big or Go Home:** Dream big! Whatever you put your mind to, you can do! Do not let anyone hold you back from your goals. In addition, do not be fearful to try new things. Think on a larger scale.

5. **Knowledge is Power:** Have you noticed how competitive the job market has become. Whatever field you wish to pursue your dream in, learn as much as you can to be an expert in it. The more you know the more you grow!

6. **Become Organized:** If you are anything like me, I need a clean environment to think properly. Cleaning the areas around you actually causes you to think clearer.

7. **Remind Yourself:** Place symbolic icons, scriptures or quotes around you. This can be on your computer, refrigerator, or somewhere to remind yourself of your goals. This also helps to remain positive.

8. **Time Management:** Schedule your day so that you have time to accomplish what is on your to do list. Controlling your time will help with procrastination.

9. **Volunteer:** If you have any extra time please please volunteer. This opportunity is so rewarding. Helping others on any level makes a person feel so much better about themselves.

10. **Motivate Others:** Motivating others actually has a reverse effect on you. Once you help push others toward their goals it is a reality check for you.

11. **Get a Buddy System:** Do you have any close friends or family members? Hold each other accountable for reaching goals. Write a bucket list together and make sure the other person goes to at least one vacation spot per year.

12. **Get a Mentor:** I am 30 years of age and still have one. Get one! They come in handy when you need an opinion or someone to talk to.

13. **Take Walks:** I love when I come home each day and take a walk. During this time, I unwind and enjoy nature. We all need a break here and there. My husband and I use this time to bond.

14. **Read Success Stories**: Rich Dad Poor Dad. I love the book. Get a copy, quick. It is a great idea to read success stories to inspire you to action.

15. **Listen to Music:** I have a great appreciation for music. I started playing the trumpet at eight years of age. Music can cool, stimulate, and sometimes sadden. What kind of music do you enjoy?

16. **Read Positive Quotes:** It may be short and simple, but quotes help. There are millions of quotes to read on a daily basis from the web.

17. **Eat a Healthy Diet**: My husband and I are vegetarians. The transition took awhile but we made it! In order to enjoy your success, you must eat a healthy diet that includes all the necessary nutrients.

18. **Sleep Sleep Sleep**: This is something I need more of! Get a full night's rest to be rejuvenated and ready to rock out the next day.

19. **Continue to Learn**: Grab a book here and there for fun. It is easy nowadays to read with the Kindle. Do your own research and find out what you are curious about. You can never get too much edification.

20. **Make Goals Specific**: Make sure the goals you write down are detailed. This is not the time to be vague or narrowed minded. You do not have to get a grade for the goals you get but do your best at listing the things your heart desires. This way they will become more attainable.

21. **Create Deadlines**: This has aided me while publishing this very book. I gave myself a deadline and I worked towards that. Setting a deadline will keep you on track and eliminate procrastination.

22. **Create a Start Date**: Just as a deadline is important; a start date is imperative as well. Write down a date to start your projects so that you will not fail to remember.

23. **Set Challenging Goals**: Make sure your goals are challenging so that you stay motivated and dedicated to achieve them. If

they are not challenging enough, you may become bored and lose enthusiasm.

24. **Make Attainable Goals:** Make sure your goals are challenging but rational. Do not expect to make 800K in week if you only make 1M per year. For those that invest in volatile stock options, this does not apply to you. You never know what the market can do.

25. **Don't Overdo It:** How many times have I done this. This is not good, at all. Do not spread yourself too thin. You should set up to three goals at a time. Anything more may be too much and usually you are unable to obtain any of the goals.

26. **Watch Your Progress:** It is a good idea to revert to your list throughout the lifecycle to make sure you are on track.

27. **Wish List:** This is one of my favorites. I love being able to list everything I want but it is even better to mark it off after I have it in my possession.

28. **Reward Yourself:** Make sure you do something nice for yourself every once in awhile. This can be treating yourself to a manicure/pedicure, dinner, shopping spree or a massage. If you accomplish a goal, celebrate! You deserve it!

29. **You Don't Always Have to Be Happy:** It is okay to be moody, especially if you are a woman. Problems will come our way. Take a break and relax!

30. **Start in the Right Direction:** Make the most out of your day and each that follows!

31. **GO TO VEGAS!** Just thought I would throw that in there.

My Much Loved Speeches of All Times!

Steve Jobs
Commencement Address 2005

Steve Jobs (1955-2011): Commence Address
Delivered 2005 Stanford University, California

When I was 17, I read a quote that went something like: "If you live each day as if it was your last, someday you'll most certainly be right." It made an impression on me, and since then, for the past 33 years, I have looked in the mirror every morning and asked myself: "If today were the last day of my life, would I want to do what I am about to do today?" And whenever the answer has been "No" for too many days in a row, I know I need to change something.

Remembering that I'll be dead soon is the most important tool I've ever encountered to help me make the big choices in life. Because almost everything—all external expectations, all pride, all fear of embarrassment or failure—these things just fall away in the face of death, leaving only what is truly important. Remembering that you are going to die is the best way I know to avoid the trap of thinking you have something to lose. You are already naked. There is no reason not to follow your heart.

Your time is limited, so don't waste it living someone else's life. Don't be trapped by dogma—which is living with the results of other people's thinking. **Don't let the noise of others' opinions drown out your own inner voice. And most important, have the courage to follow your heart and intuition.** They somehow already know what you truly want to become. Everything else is secondary.

No one wants to die. Even people who want to go to heaven don't want to die to get there. And yet death is the destination we all share. No one has ever escaped it. And that is as it should be, because Death is very likely the single best invention of Life. It is Life's change agent. It clears out the old to make way for the new. Right now the new is you, but someday not too long from now, you will gradually become the old and be cleared away. Sorry to be so dramatic, but it is quite true.

When I was young, there was an amazing publication called *The Whole Earth Catalog*, which was one of the bibles of my generation. It was created by a fellow named Stewart Brand not far from here in Menlo Park, and he brought it to life with his poetic touch. This was in the late 1960's, before personal computers and desktop publishing, so it was all made with typewriters, scissors, and Polaroid cameras. It was sort of like Google in paperback form, 35 years before Google came along: it was idealistic, and overflowing with neat tools and great notions.

Stewart and his team put out several issues of *The Whole Earth Catalog*, and then when it had run its course, they put out a final issue. It was the mid-1970s, and I was your age. On the back cover of their final issue was a photograph of an early morning country road, the kind you might find yourself hitchhiking on if you were so adventurous. Beneath it were the words: "Stay Hungry. Stay Foolish." It was their farewell message as they signed off. Stay Hungry. Stay Foolish. And I have always wished that for myself. And now, as you graduate to begin anew, I wish that for you.

Stay Hungry. Stay Foolish.

Martin Luther King Jr.
"I Have a Dream Speech August 1963

Martin Luther King Jr. (1929-1968): I Have a Dream Speech
Delivered 1963 **Martin Luther King's Address at March,**
Washington D.C.

Go back to Mississippi, go back to Alabama, go back to South Carolina, go back to Georgia, go back to Louisiana, go back to the slums and ghettos of our northern cities, knowing that somehow this situation can and will be changed. Let us not wallow in the valley of despair.

I say to you today, my friends, so even though we face the difficulties of today and tomorrow, I still have a dream. It is a dream deeply rooted in the American dream.

I have a dream that one day this nation will rise up and live out the true meaning of its creed: "We hold these truths to be self-evident: that all men are created equal."

I have a dream that one day on the red hills of Georgia the sons of former slaves and the sons of former slave owners will be able to sit down together at the table of brotherhood.

I have a dream that one day even the state of Mississippi, a state sweltering with the heat of injustice, sweltering with the heat of oppression, will be transformed into an oasis of freedom and justice.

I have a dream that my four little children will one day live in a nation where they will not be judged by the color of their skin but by the content of their character.

I have a dream today.

I have a dream that one day, down in Alabama, with its vicious racists, with its governor having his lips dripping with the words of interposition and nullification; one day right there in Alabama, little black boys and black girls will be able to join hands with little white boys and white girls as sisters and brothers.

I have a dream today.

I have a dream that one day every valley shall be exalted, every hill and mountain shall be made low, the rough places will be made plain, and the crooked places will be made straight, and the glory of the Lord shall be revealed, and all flesh shall see it together.

This is our hope. This is the faith that I go back to the South with. With this faith we will be able to hew out of the mountain of despair a stone of hope. With this faith we will be able to transform the jangling discords of our nation into a beautiful symphony of brotherhood. With this faith we will be able to work together, to pray together, to struggle together, to go to jail together, to stand up for freedom together, knowing that we will be free one day.

This will be the day when all of God's children will be able to sing with a new meaning, "My country, 'tis of thee, sweet land of liberty, of thee I sing. Land where my fathers died, land of the pilgrim's pride, from every mountainside, let freedom ring."

And if America is to be a great nation this must become true. So let freedom ring from the prodigious hilltops of New Hampshire. Let freedom ring from the mighty mountains of New York. Let freedom ring from the heightening Alleghenies of Pennsylvania!

Let freedom ring from the snowcapped Rockies of Colorado!

Let freedom ring from the curvaceous slopes of California!

But not only that; let freedom ring from Stone Mountain of Georgia!

Let freedom ring from Lookout Mountain of Tennessee!

Let freedom ring from every hill and molehill of Mississippi. From every mountainside, let freedom ring.

And when this happens, when we allow freedom to ring, when we let it ring from every village and every hamlet, from every state and every city, we will be able to speed up that day when all of God's children, black men and white men, Jews and Gentiles, Protestants and Catholics, will be able to join hands and sing in the words of the old Negro spiritual, "Free at last! free at last! thank God Almighty, we are free at last!"

John Walsh

Commencement Address 2000

John Walsh: Commence Address

Delivered 2000 Wheaton College, Illinois

1. Put the alarm clock in the bathroom. (And keep the door open,) This can be ignored by those of you whose irrepressible need to get going in the morning make it unnecessary. Others—I promise!—will find it the most important thing I have to say this afternoon.

2. Do one thing at a time. Give each experience all your attention. Try to resist being distracted by other sights and sounds, other thoughts and tasks, and when it is, guide your mind back to what you are doing.

Longo before we taught "multi-tasking" to machines, I was brought up with some crude prototype Windows software in my head. I usually ran several programs at once, clicking back and forth, and always looking for a pull-down menu of new distractions. What's more, I thought that virtuosity would be a social advantage to me—the ability to impress people by doing many things at once, none of them very well. And there were a lot of things: in high school I thought I'd be admired for switching effortlessly from Calypso lyrics to baseball statistics, to Latin, to brands of single malt whiskey. In graduate school, I met my ideal in life when I studied the career of the Flemish painter Peter Paul Roberts, who was described by a Danish man who visited Rubens at work in his studio in the 1630s in Antwerp:

"While he was still painting, [Rubens] was having Tacitus read aloud to him, and was dictating a letter. When [we were] silent so we wouldn't disturb him, he began to talk to us, while continuing to paint, listening to the reading, and dictating his letter, answering our questions and thus displaying his astonishing powers."

A few geniuses can succeed this way; most of us can't and shouldn't try. I am not warning against learning many things on many subjects, and virtuosity can indeed be useful. My warning is against distraction; whether you invite it or just let it happen, as I have done all my life. In baseball, high-percentage hitters know better: it's "focus" they talk about, and they prize it as much as strength. Psychologists describe skilled rock climbers and tennis players and pianists as going beyond focus, to what they have called a "flow" experience, a sense of absorption with the rock or the ball or the music in which the "me versus it" disappears and there's a kind of oneness with the task that brings a joyful higher awareness, as well as successful performance. I have had these experiences, too little but not too late, and probably you have, too. They are a supreme kind of pleasure. You will have more of them if you do one thing at a time.

3. Spend more time listening. Lawyers have a saying about conferences between legal opponents: "The side doing the talking is losing," For the longest time I thought that the test of my value was what I had to say. When I was not talking, I did listen to others, but with half my mind figuring out what I would say next. It is as though I had been listening to music and just registering the melody but not hearing the harmony, the instruments, the subtleties of phrasing. To really listen takes active attention. To have listened and absorbed the whole message, with all its connotations, its unspoken and maybe unintended shadings, makes it likelier that when you do speak, you will contribute more, and do so with fewer words.

4. Make yourself clear. This is risky. To say clearly what you think is to risk being more clearly wrong. To fudge what you think—to qualify it, complicate it, and overload it—is usually a defensive move. It is a strategy for getting partial credit: you figure you may be wrong but at least you are clever, you are eloquent . . . and maybe not that far wrong.

I work in a field—art history—that is rich in adjectives, poor in provable statements, just right for somebody who hides from clarity behind vivid, entertaining language. The best antidote I ever heard prescribed to writers came from the art historian Howard Hibbard, who told us students what to do when we had written a sentence: "Take your favorite word and strike it out." Hibbard meant that often we put the word there not for clarity but for vanity.

Now that I have been spending most of my time as a manager, by the way, clarity has become a necessity, and my best friend. It saves my time and other people's. As to the risk of clarity I mentioned just now, that is mostly imaginary; after all, I do still have my job.

5. You educate yourself. From now on, you had better put yourself in charge of your own education, if you have not already, you may have to buck the system. American graduate education is a lot more clearly structured and scheduled than its British and European models. The menu and the timetable are there in the catalogue: take your choice of degree programs, sign up, take the courses, pass the exams, write the thesis, and out you come—certified—a doctor, lawyer, art historian, computer scientist, and philosopher. Along the way, most graduate programs confine you to the professional cultures you are preparing to enter. In medicine and law, do not expect to be taught much about the minds and spirits of the people you are preparing to serve. In the humanities and social sciences, everything will conspire to keep you close to the library and the computer, and away from the real subject of your study, whether it is Renaissance paintings, or the Balkans, or family farmers.

6. Learn to draw. Or to play the cello. Or to tap dance, Something impractical, even useless. Whatever it is, it ought to be hard for you, something you do not really have time for, and that by professional standards you probably won't ever do well. I recommend drawing because when you get it right, maybe only occasionally, you will have such amazing waves of surprise and joy. And I promise that you'll have always be able to draw on a personal insight, a visceral empathy, with centuries of artists and their struggles to get it right.

7. Keep a journal. For many people this is harder than tap dancing. Knowing you're going to write something every day sharpens your attention to everything that happens, With a journal, you have this companion you're going to point things out to, so you stockpile impressions and passing thoughts, or, if you have a fitful memory like mine, you jot down notes to yourself It's good to begin with modest expectations—a spiral notebook from the drugstore, not a leather-bound diary with little red ribbon. Limit the time you spend at it, but do it every day. When you fail, start again. Again. For the longest time, I did not keep a journal, and as a result, much of my pretty long and interesting life is lost to me. That is a waste, one that you need not let happen to you.

8. You will be more like your parents than you imagine, or want to be. One morning at the age of 45, I looked in the mirror to shave and there was my father looking back at me. Around the same time, my

kids started noticing that I was sounding like my mother, and even now, Jill helpfully points out that when conversation gets tedious or embarrassing, I tend to leave the room—just like my mother. Now I notice I have Dad's speech mannerisms and his walk, and my closet has his smells. My parents are both dead now, and there are days when I feel that I am not just like my parents, I am my parents. Something like this will happen to you, but it need not creep up on you and surprise you. Many of your parents have made sacrifices to give you the chance to be different from them, including send you to Wheaton, and of course you may be even more different as time passes. At some point, though, you will discover your similarities, count on it. To sharpen the irony, the qualities in your parents that annoy you today are likely to be exactly the ones that, later on, your kids will point out in you. So, until then, try giving your parents a break and have a sense of humor about all their qualities.

Obama Inaugural Address
20th January 2009

My fellow citizens:

I stand here today humbled by the task before us, grateful for the trust you have bestowed, mindful of the sacrifices borne by our ancestors. I thank President Bush for his service to our nation, as well as the generosity and cooperation he has shown throughout this transition.

Forty-four Americans have now taken the presidential oath. The words have been spoken during rising tides of prosperity and the still waters of peace. Yet, every so often the oath is taken amidst gathering clouds and raging storms. At these moments, America has carried on not simply because of the skill or vision of those in high office, but because We the People have remained faithful to the ideals of our forbearers, and true to our founding documents.

So it has been. So it must be with this generation of Americans.

That we are in the midst of crisis is now well understood. Our nation is at war, against a far-reaching network of violence and hatred. Our economy is badly weakened, a consequence of greed and irresponsibility on the part of some, but also our collective failure to make hard choices and prepare the nation for a new age. Homes have been lost; jobs shed; businesses shuttered. Our health care is too costly; our schools fail too many; and each day brings further evidence that the ways we use energy strengthen our adversaries and threaten our planet.

These are the indicators of crisis, subject to data and statistics. Less measurable but no less profound is a sapping of confidence across our land—a nagging fear that America's decline is inevitable, and that the next generation must lower its sights.

Today I say to you that the challenges we face are real. They are serious and they are many. They will not be met easily or in a short span of time. But know this, America—they will be met.

On this day, we gather because we have chosen hope over fear, unity of purpose over conflict and discord.

On this day, we come to proclaim an end to the petty grievances and false promises, the recriminations and worn out dogmas, that for far too long have strangled our politics.

We remain a young nation, but in the words of Scripture, the time has come to set aside childish things. The time has come to reaffirm our enduring spirit; to choose our better history; to carry forward that precious gift, that noble idea, passed on from generation to generation: the God-given promise that all are equal, all are free, and all deserve a chance to pursue their full measure of happiness.

In reaffirming the greatness of our nation, we understand that greatness is never a given. It must be earned. Our journey has never been one of short-cuts or settling for less. It has not been the path for the faint-hearted—for those who prefer leisure over work, or seek only the pleasures of riches and fame. Rather, it has been the risk-takers, the doers, the makers of things—some celebrated but more often men and women obscure in their labor, who have carried us up the long, rugged path towards prosperity and freedom.

For us, they packed up their few worldly possessions and traveled across oceans in search of a new life.

For us, they toiled in sweatshops and settled the West; endured the lash of the whip and plowed the hard earth.

For us, they fought and died, in places like Concord and Gettysburg; Normandy and Khe Sahn.

Time and again these men and women struggled and sacrificed and worked till their hands were raw so that we might live a better life. They saw America as bigger than the sum of our individual ambitions; greater than all the differences of birth or wealth or faction.

This is the journey we continue today. We remain the most prosperous, powerful nation on Earth. Our workers are no less productive than when this crisis began. Our minds are no less inventive, our goods and services no less needed than they were last week or last month or last year. Our capacity remains undiminished. But our time of standing pat, of protecting narrow interests and putting off unpleasant decisions—that time has surely passed. Starting today, we must pick ourselves up, dust ourselves off, and begin again the work of remaking America.

For everywhere we look, there is work to be done. The state of the economy calls for action, bold and swift, and we will act—not only to create new jobs, but to lay a new foundation for growth. We will build the roads and bridges, the electric grids and digital lines that feed our commerce and bind us together. We will restore science to its rightful place, and wield technology's wonders to raise health care's quality and lower its cost. We will harness the sun and the winds and the soil to fuel our cars and run our factories. And we will transform our schools and colleges and universities to meet the demands of a new age. All this we can do. And all this we will do.

Now, there are some who question the scale of our ambitions—who suggest that our system cannot tolerate too many big plans. Their memories are short. For they have forgotten what this country has already done; what free men and women can achieve when imagination is joined to common purpose, and necessity to courage.

What the cynics fail to understand is that the ground has shifted beneath them—that the stale political arguments that have consumed us for so long no longer apply. The question we ask today is not whether our government is too big or too small, but whether it works—whether it helps families find jobs at a decent wage, care they can afford, a retirement that is dignified. Where the answer is yes, we intend to move forward. Where the answer is no, programs will end. And those of us who manage the public's dollars will be held to account—to spend wisely, reform bad habits, and do our business in the light of day—because only then can we restore the vital trust between a people and their government.

Nor is the question before us whether the market is a force for good or ill. Its power to generate wealth and expand freedom is unmatched, but this crisis has reminded us that without a watchful eye, the market can spin out of control—and that a nation cannot prosper long when it favors only the prosperous. The success of our economy has always depended not just on the size of our Gross Domestic Product, but on the reach of our prosperity; on the ability to extend opportunity to every willing heart—not out of charity, but because it is the surest route to our common good.

As for our common defense, we reject as false the choice between our safety and our ideals. Our Founding Fathers, faced with perils we can scarcely imagine, drafted a charter to assure the rule of law and the rights of man, a charter expanded by the blood of generations. Those ideals still light the world, and we will not give them up for expedience's sake. And so to all other peoples and governments who are watching today, from the grandest capitals to the small village where my father was born: know that America is a friend of each nation and every man, woman, and child who seeks a future of peace and dignity, and we are ready to lead once more.

Recall that earlier generations faced down fascism and communism not just with missiles and tanks, but with the sturdy alliances and enduring convictions. They understood that our power alone cannot protect us, nor does it entitle us to do as we please. Instead, they knew that our power grows through its prudent use; our security emanates from the justness of our cause, the force of our example, the tempering qualities of humility and restraint.

We are the keepers of this legacy. Guided by these principles once more, we can meet those new threats that demand even greater effort—even greater cooperation and understanding between nations. We will begin to responsibly leave Iraq to its people, and forge a hard-earned peace in Afghanistan. With old friends and former foes, we'll work tirelessly to lessen the nuclear threat, and roll back the specter of a warming planet. We will not apologize for our way of life, nor will we waver in its defense, and for those who seek to advance their aims by inducing terror and slaughtering innocents, we say to you now that our spirit is stronger and cannot be broken; you cannot outlast us, and we will defeat you.

For we know that our patchwork heritage is a strength, not a weakness. We are a nation of Christians and Muslims, Jews and Hindus—and non-believers. We are shaped by every language and culture, drawn from every end of this Earth; and because we have tasted the bitter swill of civil war and segregation, and emerged from that dark chapter stronger and more united, we cannot help but believe that the old hatreds shall someday pass; that the lines of tribe shall soon dissolve; that as the world grows smaller, our common humanity shall reveal itself; and that America must play its role in ushering in a new era of peace.

To the Muslim world, we seek a new way forward, based on mutual interest and mutual respect. To those leaders around the globe who seek to sow conflict, or blame their society's ills on the West—know that your people will judge you on what you can build, not what you destroy. To those who cling to power through corruption and deceit and the silencing of dissent, know that you are on the wrong side of history; but that we will extend a hand if you are willing to unclench your fist.

To the people of poor nations, we pledge to work alongside you to make your farms flourish and let clean waters flow; to nourish starved bodies and feed hungry minds. And to those nations like ours that enjoy relative plenty, we say we can no longer afford indifference to the suffering outside our borders; nor can we consume the world's resources without regard to effect. For the world has changed, and we must change with it.

As we consider the road that unfolds before us, we remember with humble gratitude those brave Americans who, at this very hour, patrol far-off deserts and distant mountains. They have something to tell us, just as the fallen heroes who lie in Arlington whisper through the ages. We honor them not only because they are guardians of our liberty, but because they embody the spirit of service; a willingness to find meaning in something greater than themselves. And yet, at this moment—a moment that will define a generation—it is precisely this spirit that must inhabit us all.

For as much as government can do and must do, it is ultimately the faith and determination of the American people upon which this nation relies. It is the kindness to take in a stranger when the levees break, the selflessness of workers who would rather cut their hours than see a friend lose their job which sees us through our darkest hours. It is the firefighter's courage to storm a stairway filled with smoke, but also a parent's willingness to nurture a child, that finally decides our fate.

Our challenges may be new. The instruments with which we meet them may be new. But those values upon which our success depends—honesty and hard work, courage and fair play, tolerance and curiosity, loyalty and patriotism—these things are old. These things are true. They have been the quiet force of progress throughout our history. What is demanded then is a return to these truths. What is required of us now is a new era of responsibility—a recognition, on the part of every American, that we have duties to ourselves, our nation, and the world, duties that we do not grudgingly accept but rather seize gladly, firm in the knowledge that there is nothing so satisfying to the spirit, so defining of our character, than giving our all to a difficult task.

This is the price and the promise of citizenship.

This is the source of our confidence—the knowledge that God calls on us to shape an uncertain destiny.

This is the meaning of our liberty and our creed—why men and women and children of every race and every faith can join in celebration across this magnificent mall, and why a man whose father less than sixty years ago might not have been served at a local restaurant can now stand before you to take a most sacred oath.

So let us mark this day with remembrance, of who we are and how far we have traveled. In the year of America's birth, in the coldest of months, a small band of patriots huddled by dying campfires on the shores of an icy river. The capital was abandoned. The enemy was advancing. The snow was stained with blood. At a moment when the outcome of our revolution was most in doubt, the father of our nation ordered these words be read to the people:

"Let it be told to the future world . . . that in the depth of winter, when nothing but hope and virtue could survive . . . that the city and the country, alarmed at one common danger, came forth to meet [it]."

America. In the face of our common dangers, in this winter of our hardship, let us remember these timeless words. With hope and virtue, let us brave once more the icy currents, and endure what storms may come. Let it be said by our children's children that when we were tested we refused to let this journey end, that we did not turn back nor did we falter; and with eyes fixed on the horizon and God's grace upon us, we carried forth that great gift of freedom and delivered it safely to future generations.

Thank you. God bless you and God bless the United States of America.

Sojourner Truth
"Ain't I a Woman?" December 1851

Sojourner Truth (1797-1883): Ain't I A Woman?
Delivered 1851
Women's Convention, Akron, Ohio

Well, children, where there is so much racket there must be something out of kilter. I think that 'twixt the negroes of the South and the women at the North, all talking about rights, the white men will be in a fix pretty soon. But what's all this here talking about?

That man over there says that women need to be helped into carriages, and lifted over ditches, and to have the best place everywhere. Nobody ever helps me into carriages, or over mud-puddles, or gives me any best place! And ain't I a woman? Look at me! Look at my arm! I have ploughed and planted, and gathered into barns, and no man could head me! And ain't I a woman? I could work as much and eat as much as a man—when I could get it—and bear the lash as well! And ain't I a woman? I have borne thirteen children, and seen most all sold off to slavery, and when I cried out with my mother's grief, none but Jesus heard me! And ain't I a woman?

Then they talk about this thing in the head; what's this they call it? [member of audience whispers, "intellect"] That's it, honey. What's that got to do with women's rights or negroes' rights? If my cup won't hold but a pint, and yours holds a quart, wouldn't you be mean not to let me have my little half measure full?

Then that little man in black there, he says women can't have as much rights as men, 'cause Christ wasn't a woman! Where did your

Christ come from? Where did your Christ come from? From God and a woman! Man had nothing to do with Him.

If the first woman God ever made was strong enough to turn the world upside down all alone, these women together ought to be able to turn it back, and get it right side up again! And now they is asking to do it, the men better let them. Obliged to you for hearing me, and now old Sojourner ain't got nothing more to say.

Serenity Prayer

God, grant me the serenity to accept the things I cannot change. The courage to change the things I can, And the wisdom to know the difference.

- ❖ **Philippians 4:6:** "Do not be anxious about anything, but in every situation, by prayer and petition, with thanksgiving, present your requests to God."
- ❖ **Matthew 28:19:** "Therefore go and make disciples of all nations, baptizing them in the name of the Father and of the Son and of the Holy Spirit."
- ❖ **John 3:16:** "For God so loved the world that he gave his one and only Son, that whoever believes in him shall not perish but have eternal life."
- ❖ **Proverbs 3:5:** "Trust in the LORD with all your heart and lean not on your own understanding."
- ❖ **Proverbs 3:6:** "In all your ways submit to him, and he will make your paths straight."
- ❖ **Romans 12:2:** "Do not conform to the pattern of this world, but be transformed by the renewing of your mind. Then you will be able to test and approve what God's will is—his good, pleasing and perfect will."

- ❖ **Romans 8:28:** "And we know that in all things God works for the good of those who love him, who have been called according to his purpose."
- ❖ **Jeremiah 29:11:** "'For I know the plans I have for you,' declares the LORD, 'plans to prosper you and not to harm you, plans to give you hope and a future.'"
- ❖ **Philippians 4:13:** "I can do all this through him who gives me strength."

References

Agrillo, C. (2011). Near-death experience: Out-of-body and out-of-brain?. *Review Of General Psychology, 15*(1), 1-10. doi:10.1037/a0021992

Baumeister, Roy F.; Vohs, Kathleen D. Snyder, C. R. (Ed); Lopez, Shane J. (Ed), (2002). The pursuit of meaningfulness in life. Handbook of positive psychology. (pp. 608-618). New York, NY, US: Oxford University Press, xviii, 829 pp.

Baumeister R. (2012). Self-control—The moral muscle. The Psychologist, Vol 25(2), Feb, 2012. pp. 112-115.

Bindley, K. (2011-12-22). Marriage rates: Divorce fears to blame for low rates? *Huffington Post*. Retrieved from http://www.huffingtonpost.com/2011/12/22/marriage-rates-divorce-fears_n_1163811.html?1324574496&icid+maing-grid7

Greyson, B., & Bush, N. E. (1996). Distressing near-death experiences. In L. W.Bailey & J.Yates (Eds.), *The near-death experience: A reader*. New York: Routledge.

Hedberg, P., Gustafson, Y., & Brulin, C. (2010). Purpose in life among men and women aged 85 years and older. *The International Journal Of Aging & Human Development, 70*(3), 213-229. doi:10.2190/AG.70.3.c

Hofmann, W., Baumeister, R.F., Foerster, G. & Vohs, K.D. (in press). Seven thousand desires: Desire, conflict, and control in everyday life. *Journal of Personality and Social Psychology*.

Mead, N.L., Baumeister, R.F., Gino, F. et al. (2009). Too tired to tell the truth: Self-control resource depletion and dishonesty. *Journal of ExperimentalSocial Psychology, 45*, 594-597.

Moody, R. A. (1975). *Life after life*. Covington, GA: Mockingbird Books.

Jordan Paul LaBouff, Wade C. Rowatt, Megan K. Johnson, Jo-Ann Tsang & Grace McCullough Willerton. Humble persons are more helpful than less humble persons: Evidence from three studies. *The Journal of Positive Psychology. Volume_7, Issue_1, 2012 pages 16-29*.

Reynaud, M., Karila, L., Blecha, L., & Benyamina, A. (2010). Is love passion an addictive disorder?. The American Journal Of Drug And Alcohol Abuse, 36(5), 261-267. doi:10.3109/00952990.2010.495183

Seligman, M.E.P. (2002). *Authentic Happiness: Using the New Positive Psychology to Realize Your Potential for Lasting Fulfillment*. New York: Free Press. ISBN 0-7432-2297-0 (Paperback edition, 2004, Free Press, ISBN 0-7432-2298-9)

References for Speeches

1. Steve Jobs Commencement Address 2005
    http://news.stanford.edu/news/2005/june15/jobs-061505.html

2. Martin Luther King Jr. "I Have a Dream Speech August 1963
    http://grammar.about.com/od/classicessays/a/dreamspeech_2.htm

3. John Walsh Commencement Address 2000
    http://www.graduationwisdom.com/speeches/0008-walsh.htm

4. Sojourner Truth "Ain't I a Woman?"
    http://www.fordham.edu/halsall/mod/sojtruth-woman.asp

5. Obama Inaugural Address 20th January 2009
    http://abcnews.go.com/Politics/Inauguration/president-obama-inauguration-speech-transcript/story?id=6689022

www.ingramcontent.com/pod-product-compliance
Lightning Source LLC
Chambersburg PA
CBHW030354290526
45785CB00004B/1746